MUTE:
Poems That Saved My Life!

Poems by Vidya Gargote during Her
Journey Battling with Depression

Vidya Gargote

BALBOA.
PRESS

A DIVISION OF HAY HOUSE

Balboa Press books may be ordered through booksellers or by contacting:

Balboa Press
A Division of Hay House
1663 Liberty Drive
Bloomington, IN 47403
www.balboapress.com
1 (877) 407-4847

Because of the dynamic nature of the Internet, any web addresses or links contained in this book may have changed since publication and may no longer be valid. The views expressed in this work are solely those of the author and do not necessarily reflect the views of the publisher, and the publisher hereby disclaims any responsibility for them.

The author of this book does not dispense medical advice or prescribe the use of any technique as a form of treatment for physical, emotional, or medical problems without the advice of a physician, either directly or indirectly. The intent of the author is only to offer information of a general nature to help you in your quest for emotional and spiritual well-being. In the event you use any of the information in this book for yourself, which is your constitutional right, the author and the publisher assume no responsibility for your actions.

Any people depicted in stock imagery provided by Thinkstock are models, and such images are being used for illustrative purposes only.
Certain stock imagery © Thinkstock.

Printed in the United States of America.

ISBN: 978-1-4525-2043-8 (sc)
ISBN: 978-1-4525-2045-2 (hc)
ISBN: 978-1-4525-2044-5 (e)

Library of Congress Control Number: 2014914750

Balboa Press rev. date: 8/26/2014

Contents

Phase 1: When All was Well 1

1. Knots 3
2. Flow 4
3. My Universe 7
4. Pay Attention 9
5. The Universal Mind 10
6. Free 11
7. Difference 12

Phase 2: Battling the blues 13

8. Believe 15
9. Honor 16
10. Peace Within Myself 17
11. Voices in My Head 19
12. Hospital Food 20
13. Broken Business 21
14. Shining Star 22
15. Good Luck 23
16. My Doctor 24
17. Friends 25
18. When I Am Rich and Famous 26
19. By Hook or By Crook 28
20. I Will Not Come with You 29
21. Love to the World 31
22. Therapy 32
23. Millionaire 35
24. Meditation 36
25. Deliverance 37

26. Accepting Reality 38

27. Half-Smile 41

28. Radical Acceptance 42

29. Every Day in Every Way I Get Better and Better 44

30. Self-Soothe 45

31. Bend the Moment 46

32. Wise Mind 49

33. Visiting Hour 50

34. Occupational Therapy 51

35. What Really Matters 52

36. Mute 53

37. Universal Prayer for Good Luck 54

38. Coexistence 55

39. The Invisible Wall 56

40. Love to be Famous 57

41. Never Settle for Good Enough 58

42. Stop Pleasing the Invisible 61

43. My Security Guards 62

44. Heal Myself 63

45. After Discharge 64

46. My Poems 65

47. My New Universe 66

48. 4/14/14 67

49. Learn to Live 68

50. Ms. Perfect 71

51. PHP 72

52. Feather on My Hat 73

53. Mirror 74

54. Me on TED.com 75

55. Three-Year-Old Parent 76

56. Dance to Radio 77

57. ACT from the Heart 78

58. Self-Care 79

59. Raising My Vibrations 81

60. I Feel So Alone 83

61. One Day at a Time 84

62. Give Up the Story 85

Phase 3: Recovery and Self-Motivation 87

63. The Believers 89

64. My Elder Sister's Wedding 91

65. Promises for My Day 92

66. Sweet and Sour 100

67. Someone Will Come Along 103

68. God Tell me Why 104

69. What Am I Doing? 108

70. I Am 109

71. When Are You Showing Me Your Grace 111

72. God Save Me 115

73. Past My Tears 119

74. How I Won a Lottery 121

75. Do You Trust Me? 123

76. Into Silence Again 125

77. Me and My Hot Ginger Tea 126

78. Potty Training My Kid 127

79. My Wish 129

80. I Found My Way 131

81. I Spoke with the Divine 132

82. No More Excuses 135

83. God, Please Help Me Transcend My Dreams 137

84. My Confidence 140

85. I Won't Fall Apart 144

86. Change Please Come 149

87. Everything Is History from Today 151

88. Where Are You, Superman? 153

89. Just Breathe 156

90. The Spring Sun 158

91. Little Girl Sitting on the Mango Tree 160

92. No More Excuses 162

93. Bully Strikes Again 164

94. Romeo Please Save Me; I Feel So Alone 165

95. The Story of the Goldfish and the Sharks 167

96. My Magic Mentor 170

97. What Are My Talents? 173

98. The Scale Has Finally Tipped 175

99. My Dear Bully 177

100. Topics to Discuss 181

101. Don't Know What to Write Today 183

102. God Grant Me the Serenity 186

103. Stupid Fat 188

104. Recovery Plan 191

105. A Beautiful Hummingbird 193

106. No Shame 194

107. Medicine 195

108. I Don't Want 196

Preface

This book is a compilation of my poems written over several years while I was battling depression. The first half of the book includes poems I wrote when I didn't even know that I was suffering with depression. I realized the difficulties in my normal life with low moods and used all available coping methods to deal with these moods, such as exercising, creative writing, and spiritual approaches like reaching out to God. I had not consulted with a doctor yet. I was under the impression that I was going through spiritual development. In many of these poems I was talking directly to God. I also reached out to the fictional superhero Superman for support and help. When I was in a really low mood, I used creative writing to get out of it. I usually imagined myself to be a little girl whom everyone loved. I exposed all my vulnerability through my poems, thinking that I was on a very grand spiritual journey and that I was guided by spirit guides and mentors.

The main turning point of the book occurred when I was hospitalized for depression, and things took a very different turn for me. Everything that I had thought about the spiritual world was shattered. I grew very upset and had to learn to live with my depression. At first I refused the illness and the medicine, but slowly the hospitalization brought me to the realization that I was in fact really sick and needed therapy. I used all my skills to radically accept that I was really depressed.

Upon this self-realization, I began my journey of recovery using all possible skills that therapy provided. I used regular medication along with the skills. It worked beautifully in my favor, and now I am getting better and better every day. Now I am living a fabulous life and coping with the disease by using skills, pills, and support groups.

This book is dedicated to all those people out there who are struggling with depression but have no idea that there is so much help available.

PHASE 1

When All was Well

Knots

One cannot deny the knots
tied by the one himself.

One cannot love oneself
without loving all the pieces of his soul.

We all reflect the same being,
and it is neither you nor me.

Everything happens for a reason.
We don't need to understand all of it.

But remember that all our connections
are originating from the divine.

Love me or hate me.
It only means you are a part of me.

We have one life to put all the pieces together,
one life to glue them with peace and harmony.

If we cannot, we are scattered.
If we succeed, we don't need to be born again.

Flow

Life is a flow,
Who am I to stop it
or direct which way to go?

Whichever way it goes,
it is always right,
because it knows

that eventually it is going to take us
exactly to the place we are destined
to be and to reach.

My Universe

You hold the world in your hands.
I hold the universe in my hands.
I am in you and you are in me.
Sometimes I think, *Who are we?*

Some days we are everything.
Some days we are nothing.
What is in between
it is neither you nor me.

Yes we are indeed divine beings.
You code the universe,
and I fill in the love.
Together we sing the verse.

Where are my angels?
Do they leave me any feathers?
No they sing to me, "Congratulations,"
and speak to me in signs.

They are all over the place,
talking to me all the time.
What is it that I am supposed to do?
Find my position in the divine universe true?

They say don't try to be special.
Be ordinary and make a mark.
But I am not made to make an ordinary mark.
I will leave a great mark or disappear like a blue shark.

There are all sorts of superbeings.
I am one among them.
The best part about it is that
people don't know about them.

Maybe I chase away the storms.
Maybe I fight the ill wills.
Maybe I mend the broken heart.
Or maybe I keep the world together.

We are all impacting the world
one emotion at a time.
We are connecting where we gather
to keep this marvelous universe together.

Pay Attention

Pay attention to what you are
paying attention to,
because you are giving your energy
to what you are paying attention to.

Let your focus be on
family and friends.
That's where your own source is.
That's where you will find your energy.

The Universal Mind

There is no we.
There is no them.
All that there is
is one mind.

One playing different roles
to different people
to teach different lessons,
remaining in perfect harmony and being equal.

There is no reason for fear.
There is no reason for regret.
There is only room for good experience,
and to take the lessons.

So do what you love to do.
Be whom you want to be.
Chase all your dreams,
using love as your means.

Life is simple.
Life is easy.
I am in love with you.
I am in love with me.

Free

I was sitting in heaven
with my eyes closed.
Seeing what was unpleasant
down on earth I descend.

Now that I am here
I will see that everyone is free
and there is no fear.
Free to dream, free to love.

free to create abundance,
free to earn glory above,
free to come into heaven.
All is well in my universe,

and all my angels are on guard
making sure everyone forgives,
filling love in every corner,
and ensuring everyone coexists.

Difference

You are fighting for greed of money and sex.
I am fighting for humanity and freedom.
We are worlds apart.
Doesn't matter if you win or I win?
We are on different tracks.

PHASE 2

Battling the blues

Believe

We need one mind so strong,
so brave, so persistent, so determined, so aggressive
to believe that we are free,
to free the entire creation.

We need one heart so sweet,
so kind, so humble, so forgiving,
so giving, so loving to give
love to the entire universe.

Let that mind and
heart be mine.
Let it be me to free humanity
and give love to all.

Honor

Never bow down to any other human being
in pain or in power.
We were all created equal,
And there is enough abundance for all people.

Never feel compelled to give up your honor
or to use it as a cover.
Yes lose your ego,
but don't lose honor until it's really over.

Peace Within Myself

As I fight with all my might
against an invisible enemy,
I take control of both sides of me.
The light and the dark shadow you see.

The dark shadow will do all the dirty work,
while the light side will bring harmony.
I gain total control on both these sides.
I set them up in harmony with no divides.

I bring peace within myself
by taking charge of both these sides.
I love them equally and
hope they vibrate at the right frequency.

I use my wise mind to start projects
and make important decisions.
I use my emotional mind to live and experience life.
Thus I always know what to do next.

Voices in My Head

Dear God: Today again the voices came.
The very first moment I woke up,
I dared to begin a battle with them,
as I know how to deal with this stir-up.

The only strategy that is working for me
is writing hate mail to them,
and I feel good and healthy to see
that the voices are gone by the p.m.

Please help me find an alternative way,
other than just running away,
to free me of these oppressing voices
who control my thoughts and won't go away.

I tried forgiving them many times,
but they continued to come.
So now my way is different fines
and hope it works for me every time.

Hospital Food

They serve breakfast before I wake up.
Pancakes, omelets, milk, and bread buns.
Always the same items on the menu.
I first ate them for fun.

But now they are no longer tasty.
I hate the smell of omelets.
Pancakes are too dry and are made hasty.
I skip them all for oatmeal.

Then comes lunch filled with salads,
broccoli boiled, and quesadilla without cheese.
This food seems to fill my stomach
but doesn't put my appetite to ease.

When it is evening and dinner arrives,
then there is daal, saag, and fruits.
I make some tea after dinner
and sip it while walking around in boots.

It's been several days with the same food.
My taste buds are almost dead,
and everything tastes so bland.
I don't like it but I still manage instead.

Broken Business

They threw me from one side to another,
singing songs and using whispers to communicate.
They made me their messenger
when I didn't even know why I ruminate.

But now I understand that this was a bunch of criminals
getting business for themselves and their associates.
They used me for all sorts of stuff and miracles,
and now they call me Queen Harmonious.

Well, Queen loves riches and authority.
If they used me they will pay with no choices
till my empty pockets fill with currency
and my mind is free of their voices.

If they love their business,
they can keep it to themselves.
If they ask for forgiveness,
I will not blow it up against itself.

Shining Star

"No more voices for me," I said
and boldly walked toward my life
with every bit of confidence spread
and with everyone to love and no strife

eager to see how my luck unfolds,
how my health improves,
and how I connect with my upholds
and those that really matter.

Every step I take I become luckier.
Every action I device I progress.
With all the people around me to support,
I find light in my darkest dreams and success.

"Alas," I say. I break open through this cage
and run into my future,
where there is light and love and no rage,
and there is abundance to secure.

Today I know better
whom to connect with or not.
I see my future
as a big and bright shining superstar.

Good Luck

I wake up to gorgeous sunshine.
I work with angels.
Everything I do is successful and divine,
and everywhere I go heaven faces.

All my wishes are instantaneously granted.
I get what I need before asking.
I focus only on that which is important
and walk toward the beautiful life everlasting.

My body reflects joy and beauty.
My children are always healthy.
My spouse is always loving and independent.
And I am blessed every day.

I find humor and patience easily.
I find and look for the best in the people.
I become famous for who I am—dreamy.
And my heart becomes kinder and peaceful.

My Doctor

She comes in after 9:30 p.m.
Then we sit and discuss
my health and recommendations.
She picks two questions to cover.

Every day she looks into my eyes
and sees my difficulty.
She is so eager to fix me and say byes
and help me with all her simplicity.

She promised me that she will
send me recovered from the voices.
I am no longer ill, and her medicines
are really good and potent.

One last day at the hospital
where I spent my time with my friends.
Tomorrow I will be out of here
all healthy and smarter.

Friends

The reason I quit my friends
was that they expected too much,
gave nothing, and made no amends.
They always used me as a crutch.

So I keep away from such people,
who are parasites and eat you from the inside,
Keep them away from my children.
Turn invisible to them when they misguide.

Once they realize their mistakes
and they beg for forgiveness,
forgive them selectively, since they betrayed.
Because one must know parasites have this likeness.

A friend is one who supports and helps
one in need and is always there
on a sunny day and on a dark stormy day.
He/she is like an invisible armor.

When I Am Rich and Famous

When I am rich and famous
I will keep all my loved ones close.
My friends will be happy for me,
and my parents can live with me.

When I am rich and famous,
I will wear false eyelashes
and hair extension of different colors.
I will be so healthy that I will smell better.

When I am rich and famous,
I will gift a real helicopter to my son.
I will have a shoe closet bigger than a room.
I will always wear designer clothes.

When I am rich and famous,
I will meet Kareena Kapoor, Barach Obama, and Oprah.
I will have home in all beautiful cities.
I will travel Europe with whole family.

When I am rich and famous,
I will have a swimming pool in my home.
My personal trainer will sculpt me.
I will have a banker who works for me.

When I am rich and famous,
we will travel to Disneyland,
enjoy every bit of its greatness,
and take full family on a cruise.

When I am rich and famous,
I will become an angel and go helping people.
I will make a difference in the world
and give to the genuine.

When I am rich and famous,
I will have an entire collection of books published.
I will own amazing mind powers
and learn how to be invisible.

When I am rich and famous,
I will make movies that will help alter the divine matrix,
educate the human mind, body, and spirit,
and soothe the soul.

By Hook or By Crook

I was an innocent girl.
but now it is not the same.
I have recognized the world
and know my place in the hall of fame.

I rule my inner world in all grandeur
and keep myself safe from thieves.
I have friends who are not mature,
and I look in the eye of fear and limiting beliefs.

For those who take from me
and dream of hurting me,
I take away everything back from them,
because there is no room for betrayal and condemn.

I keep away from magicians
and learn to live free of them.
I learn all the mind sciences
to keep myself safe.

I Will Not Come with You

When I gave you all of mine,
you stole the shiny pieces of me
and left me half dead between vultures.
So I will not come with you.

When I gave you all my love,
you found it amusing and funny.
You made me cry by your constant criticism.
So I will not come with you.

There was a time when I loved you for you.
I didn't criticize or bring you down.
I made you love yourself and be happy.
So I will not come with you.

You broke my heart so many times.
Like every other girl you used me,
and you didn't give attention to what I felt.
So I will not come with you.

I knew what you wanted.
I still gave you that along with my forgiveness.
But you are just into too many things.
So I will not come with you.

You have a list of girls whom you can run to,
and I am not like that,
because I don't believe in keeping options.
So I will not come with you.

Love to the World

So when I won all the battles
on my way home,
I stopped and wondered.
Now is the time I give my love to the world.

After all this crying and fighting,
nothing really changes on the outside.
All that changes is inside of me,
and I feel to give love to the world.

Sometime when I am afraid and lonely
and nothing really pleases me,
I stop and wonder.
Now is the time to give love to the world.

When I don't know who my friends are
or know where to look,
I stop and wonder.
Now is the time to give love to the world.

Therapy

Hey, I have been fighting all by myself
only to realize that it's too tough.
Someone said that there is therapy.
Why don't you take it?

So I explore therapy
and wonder what it will take
to clear years of depression
and help my life recover and remake.

There are numerous pills,
and there are many skills
that I need to use
to fight against this monster's abuse.

I consciously keep away from
all the triggers that hurt me.
And am not afraid of anything,
since the whole world belongs to me.

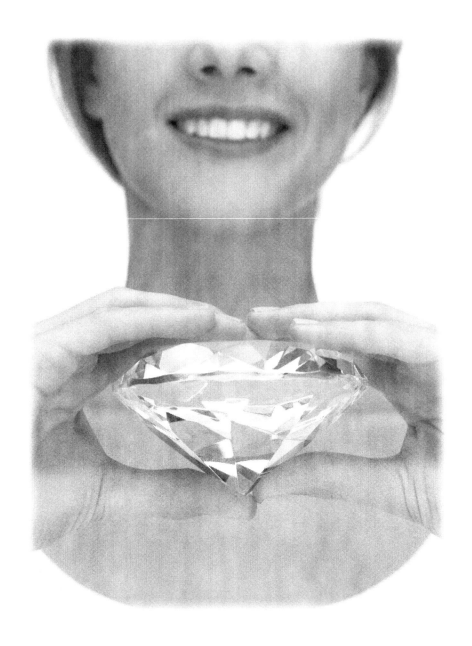

34

Millionaire

When all my plans fell flat,
when I understood that
the universe knows only to take,
I decided to keep my eyes on the ball.

At first I only wanted to be great
and have my name in history,
but now I understand myself better.
I want to be a millionaire.

I gave a lot of love and
fulfilled the dreams of millions.
I now want to focus on my goals.
I want to be a millionaire.

It's very clear how I will do it.
I will write a book and publish it.
A movie will be made based on the book
and touch the heart of millions.

Meditation

When I am writing, I am meditating.
When I am singing, I am meditating.
When I am dancing, I am meditating.
When I am relaxing, I am meditating.

So what is meditation really?
Is it that stillness of our being?
Is it the calmness of our mind?
It is the exercise of our body?

Here's my take on it:
Meditation is something that
pacifies the mind and recharges the brain.
It is self-soothing gift.

Every time I meditate,
I find something new about myself.
Sometimes it elevates my mood.
Sometimes it helps me relax.

Deliverance

Ever since I went into the hospital
I hear this word in my mind.
To me it means taking action possible,
and that's what I mean by deliverance.

So I have this gift to bring peace
and harmony in the world by writing,
by bringing important issues to notice,
and that's what I mean by deliverance.

The ultimate universal force said,
"Go ahead; do what you love.
and pursue your passion,"
and that's what I mean by deliverance.

What does it mean to take action?
It means start where I am and
do what I can and finish what I have started,
And that's what I mean by deliverance.

Accepting Reality

I see myself on the high-speed motorbike
with skin-tight leather jeans
and long shiny hair
and the looks of an angel.

I see myself acting in a movie.
The movie wins an Oscar,
and I have all that I need
and cherish as an actor and author.

I see myself being a great leader
whose speech touches the heart of millions,
who brings victory to mankind
and kills all ignorance.

I see myself writing books
and shifting the mass consciousness
and see the creativity inside me
to publish these best sellers.

Half-Smile

When all that I can do
is smile at my life
and keep walking ahead,
I choose to half-smile.

When it is so difficult to
keep up with my activities
and keep up with my chores,
I choose to half-smile.

When the sink is full of dishes
and there are three loads of washed clothes
and the dining table is full of toys,
I choose to half-smile.

When I knowingly isolate myself
from family and friends
and I withdraw into my own shell,
I choose to half-smile.

Radical Acceptance

I accept that
>> I am not innocent anymore,
>> I am not very friendly,
>> I am sometimes rude and arrogant,
>> and these are a part of my personality.

I accept that
>> I am seeking money,
>> I am seeking greatness,
>> I am seeking true friends,
>> and I am not guilty anymore.

I accept that
>> I can be a vicious hurricane,
>> I can be a smoldering volcano,
>> I can be a monster,
>> and yet I know all this is changing

I accept that
>> this is my universe.
>> Although heavier beyond my capacity,
>> I will have to manage it
>> and bring harmony inside it.

I accept that
>> even though medicine is not the best option,
>> I will stay on it.
>> I will complete the course
>> and make friends with it.

I accept that

     therapy is slow.

     I will make friends with the therapist.

     I will make friends with the psychiatrist.

     and heal every day with this support.

I accept that

     I might meet with some weirdoes.

     I will continue to find a support group,

     use this for my betterment,

     and understand myself.

Every Day in Every Way I Get Better and Better 29

Ever since I was a little girl,
I knew that I was meant to be great.
So I decided to learn something new every day.

I left no page unturned in the self-help books.
I practiced every skill that I could digest
and remembered to keep learning.

I manifested absolutely beautiful dreams.
I learned my way in the dark world
and tested everything I learned.

If the rules worked, I used them often.
If not, I discarded them
and read beautiful books to keep my mind fresh.

I followed only great people
and those whom I absolutely adored,
and thus I became better with every day.

Self-Soothe

There are days when things don't go my way
Everyone seems to be upset me,
and I am browsing the painful past dismay.

It is then when I use my self-soothing skills.
I watch a comedy movie.
I grab some sunshine
and take some pictures.
I listen to my favorite songs.
I put up a scented candle.
I make a chai tea.
I hug my dear ones.
I compose some poetry!

Bend the Moment

31

Every now and then there comes a moment
    that explodes emotions
    like a huge bomb.

I bend this moment by using one of the techniques below.
    I take one thing at a time.
    I relax and encourage myself.
    I pray to God for help.
    I imagine beautiful scenery.
    I find a deep meaning to what happened.
    I plan a vacation.

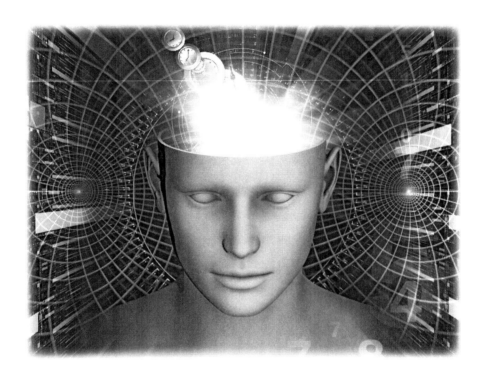

Wise Mind

32

Humans have access to three minds.
We think from the logical mind.
We experience life from the emotional mind.
But the best part of our mind
is the intersection of the logical and emotional,
and this is the wise mind.

With this wise mind we make better decisions.
We always focus on the achievement.
We keep ourselves alert and calm,
and this helps our life and intuition.

It helps us resolve our problems.
It appreciates our hard work.
It learns from mistakes
and reapplies our lessons.

Visiting Hour

It has been seven days that I have been here.
Today was Sunday, and I was all excited.
My husband came during visiting hours,
and it was so different and delightful.

We both went to my room.
He asked me if I'd eaten.
I said no, and so he opened his box of goodies:
idlis, dosas, and vadas.

After we ate he asked me if I'd washed my hair.
I said yes, and he pulled me closer
and combed my hair and tied it up
And gave me a Spiderman kiss.

When love is so much healing,
how come it is not served on the menu?
I wished I'd spend more time
with him during visiting hours.

Occupational Therapy 34

Every day at the hospital
after lunch hour we gathered
to create something new
with the radio music rapper.

The supplies included stencils,
colors, paper, glue, and accessories.
Once we made a picture frame,
a greeting card, and a glass painting of berries.

We also made a magic box,
a scratch-on poster, and some paintings.
It is so calming to cut and create props.
It definitely soothes our moods and feelings.

Sometimes we get to keep our creations.
Sometimes they are kept in our cubby.
All in all a very helpful hour of elation
reminding us of our creativity.

What Really Matters

I thought and thought.
I read books and autobiographies.
I talked to men, women, and children a lot.
I found this common --love is the quality.

And at the end of the day,
it doesn't matter who did what.
All that matters is what we took right away,
either a lesson or failure in our gut.

When nothing seems to work,
we look up to God and our loved ones
to protect us and love us,
and that's what really matters.

We keep going through these motions,
learning our lessons, and making speedy progress,
manifesting our desires with fun ease,
and that's what really matters.

Mute

I feel so blessed after the voices are gone.
What an ultimate peace in my mind.
I can now think clearly
without the voices interfering.

I had assumed that the voices will remain.
But my doctor drove them away.
I feel free and relaxed,
and there is no reason for me to worry.

Thank you God for this peaceful moment.
Thank you doctor for the exact medicine.
Thank you support group for motivation.
Thank you family for so much love.

I am finally happy
after the torture of the voices.
I am able to think clearly
and enjoy my freedom.

Universal Prayer
for Good Luck

As we enter a new age of freedom
where life is full of abundance
and relationships are full of love and reason,
I pray to the universe for good luck.

Let my universe be open to all
the people who work hard toward it.
May there be success and fame
to all the people who work for it.

Let my universe be gentle to the kind
and rude to the harsh.
May people get what they aspire in mind
and good luck be bestowed upon all.

As we all fight with the enemy for a cause,
let the universe be open to support the cause.
Let there be peace and harmony
in my universe of good luck.

Coexistence

Let the haves coexist with the don't haves.

Let each religion coexist with the other religions.

Let each country coexist with other countries.

Let the rich coexist with the poor.

Let the educated coexist with the uneducated.

Let the men coexist with the women.

Let belief systems coexist with other belief systems.

Let the societies coexist with other societies.

Let our children coexist with their children.

Let consciousness coexist with ignorance.

Let the light coexist with the dark.

When all this happens, there will be divine peace.

The Invisible Wall

After clearing all the voices,
I want to protect my head
from thieves and enemies,
so I erect an invisible wall.

This invisible wall will keep me safe.
Only those who genuinely love me will
be able to pass through this wall,
so I erect this invisible wall.

I don't really know who I love
because I only hear their voices.
I don't see anyone,
leaving it to my heart to decide.

I have given lotsa love to all,
but now I feel different.
Now I need love and hope
my heart makes the right decision.

Love to be Famous

My poems written will be published.
Some of them will be included in the movies.
Some of them will make it to Taylor Swift and Katy Perry
and other music artists.
Thus my words and poems will reach
the entire world.
I will smile and say, "I am so great."
I love to spread my words
of love and endurance,
of hope and greatness,
and sometimes because I just love to be famous.

Never Settle for Good Enough

We all go through crossroads
where we need to pick a side
and start the journey of codes.
But I have a different take alright.

No matter how late it gets
I will choose the path
that is the best for my progress
and follow the divine guidance.

Because I have had too many wrong choices,
now I love and care for myself.
I don't worry where I need to be beside this,
as I know that I am exactly where I need to be.

I have learned from my mistakes
never to settle for good enough,
always do my best,
and leave the rest to God.

Stop Pleasing
the Invisible

Every time they put me into a new movie
and let me play the role by the rules,
they expect me to be the dumb righteous heroine
and push me to my limits.

Today I realized that
there is no point in pleasing the invisible;
rather do exactly what I want
and do not worry about the consequences.

Let the invisible threaten someone else.
I am not scared of it anymore.
Let it do its duty.
I do mine without worry.

If it scares me one more time,
I will set fire to the invisible
and enjoy the fireworks
from my view.

My Security Guards

The people appointed to speed up my growth
were the ones who stole from me.
They passed my soul from one to another
and kept me empty wasting my time.

Tonight God will know everything
that they used me to create
without even asking my permission.
These are just parasites for sure.

Tonight all their plans will be exposed
and they will be blown up
Anything created by my enemy
will be destroyed and disposed.

They can never be my guards,
because they don't respect my being.
They treat me like a magic wand
that can be used for anything.

Heal Myself

Dear mind,

      Please heal my depression.

      Please heal my brain.

      Please heal my body.

      Please heal my soul.

      Please heal my spirit.

Dear mind,

      Please give back my sickness to those who gave it to me.

      Please give back everything negative I am holding on to.

      Please return this disease back to the rightful owner.

      Please send back all the spells to the appropriate owner.

After Discharge

Once I am out of this therapy
I will move myself into another universe
where relationships are real
And the world is friendlier.

First things first: I will find a job,
make some new friends,
publish my book on top,
and write a universal prayer.

I will keep away from people who belittle me.
I will find support groups,
Increase my exercise,
and eat healthy like the troops,
finish the projects I have started,
take back everything from
people who hurt me,
and raise healthy boundaries.

My Poems

Dear God, let my creativity flow
through this pen, and may I capture
every word to represent this moment.

May my poems help millions of people
also recover from self-doubt
and depression without medication.

May these poems touch the heart
of everyone who has been hurt,
build in them self-assurance and confidence.

May my poems teach persistence,
victory, joy, and healthy recovery,
and above all divine love to everyone.

My New Universe

My new universe is
> more friendly,
> more forgiving,
> more loving,
> more sharing,
> more action oriented,
> more appreciative,
> more real,
> more encouraging,
> more calm,
> more progressive,
> more happy,
> more lucky,
> more abundant,
> more blessed,
> more safe.

4/14/14

Today seems to be a lucky day for me.
I got discharged from the hospital.
Now I can live my life and drink tea
however I wish to and be unstoppable.

Free to do whatever I choose.
Free to write poems or refuse.
Free to walk in the sunshine.
Free to drive with loud music on.

Got my discharge papers.
Got my instructions for medication.
Got all the questions answered.
Got hugs and blessings and cooperation.

Tonight I am going to call upon my guardian angel
and ask him what is next for me
and to please provide me guidance
to catch up with my life again.

Learn to Live

Several days in the hospital,
several days in therapy,
to beat this depression
and to learn how to live.

Lot of skills to carry
and lot of pills to digest,
all to make myself happy
and to learn how to live.

Things are different now.
I know my power better.
I understand that I am always in control
and there is nothing to worry about.

What I need to learn is
how to keep my head up high
when things don't go my way
and how to half-smile.

Ms. Perfect

I found myself justifying
each and every emotion
as if someone were taking away
my "Ms. Perfect" medal.

But after this episode
I found out that
life is much more easier
without the medal I excel at.

It feels like the whole world
belongs to me.
And I don't need to justify my life
to anyone or give a guarantee.

Instead of being a stuffed animal,
I can be alive and jumping
around and celebrating life
without holding onto grudges.

PHP

So after the discharge I went into PHP—
partial hospitalization program—
the most boring part of the recovery.
But I still joined it.

Second day, and I am happy
I joined the program.
I got my questions answered,
and I am relieved that I came.

Feather on My Hat

My friends complimented
me today for my speech.
One said I could be a church reader.
One said I was eloquent.

I love to hear compliments.
It makes me feel I exist
And that I am appreciated
And I belong and persist.

This compliment reminded me
of a long-lost dream
where I go on the TED stage
and send a message to the entire universe.

Mirror

My heart is a mirror.
It reflects everything it gets.
If love is sent, it reflects love.
If hate is sent, it reflects hate.

It never really discriminates.
It is warm to the kind,
and it is cold to the harsh.
It all depends on what is sent.

Me on TED.com

Here is one of my dreams:
to appear on the TED stage
and talk to the world
of things that really matter in this age.

I already have a great voice.
I can read eloquently.
All I need is a chance
and a great topic of presidency.

When I am on this stage
before various intellectuals,
I mesmerize the audience
with all that I have is invaluable.

Three-Year-Old Parent

When healing my wounds
I came across a three-year-old
who found herself
moving big mountains all alone.

She always thought that
she could fix anything and anyone.
But she was just a child
with a solid upbringing.

She's like Atlas
trying to lift the entire world
but had shrugged
because of the load.

I say to the little girl,
"Drop the weight,
and focus on your well-being
Leave the world for others to hold."

Dance to Radio

Here is a habit
that has helped me
stay sane and enthusiastic.
It is dancing to the radio music.

I wake up in the morning,
finish my chores,
get my kid ready for school for learning,
and jump into my car with radio stars.

I listen to songs that
lift my spirit and mood.
I make dance moves
sitting strapped in my seat.

This beautiful habit that brings me joy,
raises my vibrations,
and soothes my mind
makes me younger every day.

ACT from the Heart

Caught a pattern in myself
of beating up myself,
of justifying to the invisible,
of expecting too much from myself.

Now releasing these chains
that caught me in my own self
and stop beating myself
to feel lighter again.

Found myself over-obsessing
over global issues
and investigating these
issues beyond my scope.

I now bring myself
into my body
and forgive myself
and quit the perfectionism.

I quit the need for approval.
I quit the need for control.
I quit the need to justify
and rebuild myself from square one.

Self-Care

58

As I slowly get into normal life,
I start eating healthy food.
I exercise regularly and break a sweat,
Push myself to do new things every day.

I get some help for my chores.
Hubby helps with daily dose of medicine.
I do grocery shopping on my own
and indulge in some great smoothies.

I get some help for my bills.
I put all my papers together,
ask my child to tidy up his room,
and have my cook care for dinners.

Remind myself that I am great mom and wife,
be awesome to myself,
forgive myself when I fail my expectations,
and stand tall and self-care.

Raising My Vibrations

As I heal from depression,
I find it very interesting
that when I raise my vibrations,
I feel better and better.

When I eat delicious food
and listen to my favorite music,
I raise my vibrations,
and I feel better and better.

When I walk in the sunshine
and when I wear my bright lipstick,
I raise my vibrations,
and I feel better and better.

When I browse through old photos
and look at baby pictures,
I raise my vibrations,
and I feel better and better.

When I drive around in my car
with loud music on,
I raise my vibrations,
and I feel better and better.

When I play badminton
or break a sweat at the gym,
I raise my vibrations,
and I feel better and better.

When I meet with my friends
and chitchat about random stuff,
I raise my vibrations,
And I feel better and better.

I Feel So Alone

Just coming out of the hospital,
And I am already feeling alone.
My new universe makes me feel
vulnerable and unknown.

I neglected all the voices
and kept away from obvious triggers.
But my chest feels sensitive
and worries about everything.

My logical mind says,
Give yourself time.
My emotional mind says,
Give your heart a break.

So I ponder over
this obvious emptiness,
and live through this episode
without getting into the hospital.

One Day at a Time

My recovery path is so huge,
but I take one day at a time.
I take baby steps
and move in the direction of light.

I keep taking my medicine
and join the support groups.
I take baby steps
and move in the direction of light.

I keep away from triggers
and people who belittle me.
I take baby steps
and move in the direction of light.

Give Up the Story

62

All of my depression is mostly
because of my personal story,
which keeps triggering me
and pulling me back into darkness.

I am ready to give up the story
if it is not working for me
or helping me recover
and write my own new story.

Let my new story
be of love and abundance,
and friends and family
and about health.

Phase 3

Recovery and Self-Motivation

The Believers

Every now and then
I look back and say,
"I did all that;
now where is my rainbow?"

I count ten steps ahead
and look back,
and see that I haven't gone too far.
I check my route thereafter.

I thought ego was the resistance.
I got rid of ego.
I changed all my thoughts
to focus only on the positive.

Yet I feel like I am
not doing enough or
pushing someone else's load.
When and what is missing?

I believe that I am doing it right
and trust my heart.
But why are these brakes on tight
when I want to fly so high?

Why do I need to look back
when I know that this is my road?
Why do thoughts come into my mind
when I don't own their load?

So here's to the army within me.
I believe that I am doing right.
I believe that I will win
all the battles I choose.

With my spirit in charge
and the whole world in my hands,
I create a unique experience
where everyone for once tastes their gifts.

Let there be joy around the world.
Let there be peace in every corner.
Let every man get what he truly deserves.
Let there be life that people aspire.

Let every soul dance to joy
and be happy and content.
Let their dreams and hopes
that add value to the world come true.

Let my hands heal every soul.
Let my words soothe the angry and depressed.
Let there be love in everyone,
and may God give me the strength to continue.

My Elder Sister's Wedding

64

There once came a man
tall, strong, and brave,
with a heart of gold and a plan
and the smartness of God.

He pulled his hand out
and stretched it out
to catch hold of my
dear elder sister's hand.

My kind sister who has
had her share of troubles
Is now relieved of all sorrows,
because there came her knight in shining armor.

Whatever she lacks he will complete.
Whatever she shares he will grow.
She will give him love and respect.
He will help her become divine.

The day is not far when my dream
shall find its way into the universe
and send down the bravest heart
to heal my kind and loving sister.

Promises for My Day

Each day when I wake up
I will see beauty in life.
I will forgive and forget negative episodes
and only keep the lesson.

I will take action
bit by bit and will always
be guided by my teachers and mentors
and discover my place in the universe.

I will develop a laser-sharp focus,
and see and do only what matters.
I will not indulge in negative thinking,
however appetizing it may be.

I will develop a strong body
and amazing shining skin and hair.
My eyes will become more beautiful,
and my mind will become smarter.

I will be able to differentiate
between friends and foe
but will always make friends who love me
and help me become God's ultimate image.

I will work out every day
and find ways to eat healthy.
I will discover nutrition
in a whole new way.

I will not let tiny setbacks
keep me from achieving
the ultimate body and mind of my dreams.
I will care for myself every day.

I will discover fashion and
change my dressing to bring out the best.
I will rediscover my beauty
every day and in every way.

I will always love back everyone
who loves me and shares my joy and bliss.
I will never undermine the goodness in me
by small talk and self-sabotage.

I will learn from my mistakes.
I will learn to be cautious
when I will be let down by tiny quarrels
with my loved ones.

My love will always find a way
to heal me and heal the one who receives it.
I will not share my love with anyone
who wants to harm me.

I will always remain composed
and not cry often,
because tears are precious
and only to be shed for valid reasons.

I will obey God's instructions.
I will love and respect him in
all forms and people I have experienced.
I will always look up to him.

I will never fail the wisdom
in my mind and heart
and seek happiness and joy
in every day's tiny moments.

I will work toward creating
something original that I can share
with the universe, and I shall
be remembered for this legacy.

My heart will never harden.
I will always find a way to profoundly
impact anyone who seeks my love.
I am human, but my love is divine.

I will learn politics only to safeguard myself,
to protect me from attacks
and help me make a way through this
infinite universe and emerge as divine.

I will act, read, and learn
every day and enrich my life with
joy and laughter,
and loneliness will never disturb me.

I will keep reminding myself
that when I take positive action,
all the universe will conspire to support me.
I will not fear to fail.

I will discover that which is keeping me restless,
that which wants to come out,
that which wants to change the entire humanity,
the unique nature and gifts bestowed upon me.

It will forever transform my life,
change my views about everything,
help me live a joyful and fulfilling life.
It will transform and bring greatness.

I will shed all my beliefs about the universe
and see everything in new light.
Everyone will have a second chance
to showcase their unique gift.

God made me from dirt,
and I will create my own universe,
which will be content and fulfilled
and full of joy and happiness

I will learn new and unique skills
and find great teachers on my way.
They will share with love
everything that I can handle.

I will find a ray of hope
even in the darkest of the day.
I will keep my face smiling and serene
and always remember who I am.

And in this theory of observation,
things only exist if we observe them.
Happiness, luck, joy, abundance, and wealth
exist and expand when we observe them.

Things, events, and negativity disappear
when you ignore them.
Nothing really exists if you don't observe,
for the world is how you perceive it.

As a mother who never stops teaching
her child to walk, so also God has
a unique way for planting experiences
in our life, to make our unique gift come to life.

The eyes that find magic in everything,
the soul that surrenders and cares,
the heart that loves
will have the keys to everything that needs to know.

Today is the day.
I decide that that will be no tears
and fears, because he cares for every drop shed
and worries if he made a mistake.

But his child will never lose confidence
in her, and she will survive
like a weed and expand
both in knowledge and in consciousness.

I will find courage and patience
and know everyone and try to see
a silver lining into every dark cloud
and renew hope and faith.

I will generate my energy from my heart,
see the world through magic glasses,
and one day will sit with him
and understand the glory of the universe.

Actions, actions, and focused action is what
my teachers are screaming at me.
Did I reach my melting point?
"Or do you need more?" God asks.

I say, "I see everything, hear everything
understand everything but will put together
my energy into action, for time is short
and dreams are big; no more confusion."

I write my own destiny.
I give energy to all those who love me.
I share my joy and love
with those I love.

My magic will transform me
into a beautiful strong woman,
strong, healthy, vibrant, charismatic,
yet very caring and tender at heart.

I will fight for a greater cause
and will always experience joy
and learning from life's unique experiences.
I will persist and survive.

I will develop a great sense of humor
and will be able to laugh at my flaws,
for we are after all human beings
and wonders in the making.

When my mind is disturbed,
I will write and compose
great pieces of thoughts
that will regenerate my energy.

I will always flow with integrative energy,
allow room for new understanding,
hope for miracles and wonders,
and take all action to build my universe.

It is my birthright to seek answers
to wonders about the universe,
to aim for the farthest
and dream for the wildest.

To rediscover, rewire my thoughts and
attitudes, my policies, practices, habits,
and change into the superhero
of my dreams.

To be the one who cares for herself
and does everything to take care
and bring out the hidden talents
and gifts mostly ignored till now.

If only they knew me better,
they would all know how much I care
for everyone, but the truth is
only when I rediscover myself.

I write to push the dark stormy clouds away
and let the sun shine bright again
on my face and my existence
and on everyone who loves me.

I gather my energy from the cosmos
and put together myself and am a brave soldier,
marching and taking action
to lead a life of happiness and bliss.

To blame is only to bring shame,
to hate is only to degenerate your soul,
to complain and worry is to nag to God,
and to cry is to defeat his confidence in you.

So I give up all these negative emotions
and learn that life can be much better
without these corrosive habits;
sooner or later they will eat the beholder.

I open myself to infinite possibilities,
listen to God through my loved ones,
obey his instructions, and keep calm;
always find courage and patience.

My story has just begun,
millions of dreams and zillions of dreams,
countless people to meet,
and infinite joy to share.

No wonder everyone calls me lucky.
Maybe I am God's second chance
to this universe and his hope
in me that I will make him proud.

Never mind the past, only the lessons
and the heartfelt love I can carry from
infinite souls who have shared life with me
because my parents gave birth to a miracle.

Sweet and Sour

Sweet and sour is the taste of life.
Discomfort and comfort are the two sides.
Why I am going through these cycles?
Because I am learning a better life.

Beauty of nature is what I enjoy.
Two moments of peace I thank.
Joy in my heart I appreciated,
and my only wish is to spend a wonderful time.

False is the illusion of wealth.
Trap is the illusion of fame.
So being aware is the only game,
and letting go of negativity is the aim.

Once I danced with appreciation,
I knew my confidence
that the only thing that really matters
is respecting myself and my universe within.

This child is reborn every time
I learn a new way to survive.
Sometimes I question even God:
What's the point of all these hurdles?

Remaining connected to the source is not easy,
because no one remembers your kindness,
and only silly acts of ego
drive your palace of cards into blindness.

Darkness sings beautiful songs
and gives me joyful moments.
But it is all a trap, I say
and make my way to sanity.

Adopt the attitude of gratitude.
It is tough but easy with patience.
Enjoy every moment as if
today were your last day on earth.

I decide from today that
I will live every day as the very last day
and enjoy every gift of mine
and share as much as I can.

God is funny, because he plays
with our minds, throws them into
troubles, and then comforts us.
Fear and greed are both his ways.

But when neither fear nor greed affects
thats where I live away from,
all those mighty illusions of wealth and fame,
man says to God, "You can take what you want,
because all is yours. Give what I deserve, and
that is it." He knows his games and his ways,
so man leaves all his cleverness and ego behind.

Who saw God; who knows him?
I didn't see him but know he is here.
Spirit is what they call, and all I know is that
sometimes he does visit me and gives my answers.

"Let there be light" is what he says.
Let your intellect shine through.
Let your nature be of giving,
and pacify your wants with your haves.

Someone Will Come Along

67

Dear God,
Separate his mind from my mind.
I cannot handle his negativity,
and he does not love me anymore.
So we are free to go our ways.

Although it is a very lonely street,
I am not afraid.
Someone will come along
and pick me up and care for me.

I need a different kind of love,
because I have to heal from
depression and low self-esteem.
This love will be warm and a shield.

God Tell me Why

Why is there uncertainty?
Why is there injustice
to your own ardent devotees
who always have done the right thing?

God tell me why
you put through fire
your loved ones, the one without
whom the world wouldn't be a better place.

God tell me why
a mother loses her baby
when he is just six days old.
Why did you give her that dream?
Why did you tear her apart?

God tell me why
you changed a smart girl
into someone who has now has doubts
about her life and dreams.

God tell me why
you put me among friends
who are like parasites,
eating everything good that's within.

God tell me why
you didn't show me the way
of not trusting them in the first place.
Why didn't you care for me?
Why didn't you bring justice?

God tell me why
even after abandoning them,
they scandalize
behind our backs?
We don't care for their sabotage.

God tell me why.
How many iterations should I go through
to find the right person as a friend?
For I know there is no one other than you
who can be my friend.

God tell me why
I gave up my job
in the midst of self-doubt and pain,
in the midst where everything nice.
It is something I cannot afford.

God tell me why
I love Oprah so much
but cannot be someone strong like her,
someone courageous like her,
fearless like her.

God tell me why
my femininity is always underappreciated,
why my spirit is undernourished,
why my soul is always reaching out to read
something that showers rains in my
field of hungry crops.

God tell me why
I hate to open up to new people.
Why do I hate to trust anymore?
Why do I hate to make new friends?
Why is my heart still bleeding
from the wounds some dark soul gave me?

God tell me why
my love for you
is all in a trash can.
Why I am the only one
you do not listen to
when I represent
not just me but
everything connected to me.

God tell me why
you do not trust me
to be the great one
you once sent to this earth.
If I cannot be one
then tell me why you gave me illusions.

God tell me why
the little girl who loved everyone,
cared for everyone,
shared with everyone,
trusted everyone, and loved everyone
is now shunning everyone.

God tell me why
you gave me faith
but you didn't give me patience.
Why you gave me love
but you took away my baby.
Why you gave me a great mind.

God tell me why
I cannot be the smart and beautiful girl
that I was once upon a time;
Why can I not heal my heart
and become the little girl
whom everyone loved.

What Am I Doing?

It's 5:52 p.m., and I am writing this
feeling anxious and in tears,
and I question what I am doing.

I wasted so much time
thinking that all will be divine,
but everything requires redesign.

I just want to give up all
and not do it again.
Looks like my pain is a game.

Game is what they played,
and I lost me in the same.
I don't know what is my name.

Lost to time
Lost to words
Lost to tears

I am done with this nonsense
of absolute hopelessness.
No more can I take.

Nothing works for me anymore.
I am lost in space
and don't know what I am doing.

I Am

As Dr. Wayne Dyer said,
"I am that I am."

Yes I am that I am,
and you are you.

But we are one,
and my tears are done.

The pain in my heart
will only remind me of you.

Tears in my eyes
will only remind me of you.

There is nothing
left of me in me.

I am that I am.
I am love.

Even if I die,
I will be reborn.

Even if I have pain,
I will heal.

If I am alone,
I will have company.

I gave you my heart
in billions of lives.

No, I don't have it with me.
I am that I am.

I am without my heart.
Because I am just love.

I don't wait for anyone
to reciprocate my love.

I cannot search anymore.
I just assume your love.

Don't ask me to prove;
just look into your heart.

I am in your heart.
No games; even if I die my love remains.

I don't search for you.
I see you in no form but just in feeling.

I merge with the infinite today
and will try to meet you in every life.

Here nothing hurts.
It's full of bliss.

And with thousands of tears
I cleanse my path to divine.

When Are You Showing Me Your Grace

71

It's 12:02 a.m., and I am writing this to you
in great spirits.

When are you going to show me your true self?
So far I saw your various forms.
Are you really there?
Or is it just another game?

Fine with me; doesn't matter.
I won't leave my search,
For what I know,
probably only a few people know.

That I have seen you;
only a part of it, not the whole.
So I search for you
all over again.

Got a secret name also.
Got a special blessing too
right in front of you.
I stood there while you blessed me.

You play hard with me.
I give it back equally well.
So I smile again.
I cannot stop smiling.

With the secret name
I am on a secret mission.
I will wipe off all the pain in the world
with my secret messages.

Come stop me and you will
be the only one to lose.
Catch me if you can.
for I am stopping for no one.

God Save Me

72

I cannot help myself anymore.
I think I have surrendered.
I cannot go on like this.

Call it depression, PMS, or feeling low or whatever.
I have hit the rock bottom.
Now I cannot get up.

My own people don't understand me.
I feel alone.
I cannot die, as I have a little one.

God, please help me.
I cannot take this pain anymore.
I am asking you to save me.

For I am so sad
that I cannot speak okay.
I am just done with all.

You know it all.
You saw me. Then why are you playing
with me so hard?

God, please bless me one more time.
Help me get through this day
without killing myself.

I may not need myself,
but my son needs me.
Please save me.

Past My Tears

73

As I think about the last three years
I cannot remember anything past my tears.
Today I felt alive again
As I got in touch with myself in pain.

We are so complicated.
When I plan to celebrate, I secretly hide my tears.
Why are we so complicated?
And all our feelings are so interconnected.

I want to throw a party
and do the usual, but my heart pulls me back.
Reminds me of the times when
we counted each second for him to survive.

So as usual we want to commemorate,
as loss and happiness both are our fate.
I ask God why this month is on the calendar.
Why do I have to remember?

But then I cannot be selfish,
for there is the little one waiting eagerly for his wish.
His wish is only of a car
which he calls "tans-fomar-car"

When I ask him how many toys he wants,
he always says five.
So went to Target today
and had him pick everything he liked.

He picked up six Hotwheels
and one green frog, a blue plane, and a monster truck.
Fun is this age
when you get your toys as well as love.

So I wish that my wish comes true
that my little one enjoys his bday that's due.
I am going to hide my tears
and get past this to make it the best day in years.

God give me your grace
and bring me a smile.
For I need to be the mother
to one and angel to another.

How I Won a Lottery

74

It's 1:56 p.m., and I am not feeling very well,
So I have to write it.

I just feel so down in the dumps,
but cannot understand what it is.
So I decide to write my story
of winning a lottery.

We were out to party
when we filled up gas.
And there was change handy.
That's when we picked up our tickets.

The numbers were random,
but I finally had reached boredom.
I cannot sit at home and do nothing,
So I write to practice winning.

Here I am writing my story
Of how I won a lottery.
For I think it's time
to see something nice.

So I feel nice when I write
this winning twice.
Yes, I am winning a lottery
tonight and hope to come out of misery.

It's 2:01 p.m., and I am done.
I feel very sad and depressed,
done with my writing,
but I will just keep moving.

Do You Trust Me?

75

It's 11:40 p.m., and I cannot sleep
without writing about it.
In the plethora of mixed signals
between the shut-offs and the goes.

I found a unique message,
and to me it said,
"Do you trust me?"
I said "yes" with all my heart.

He asked me to tell my story
of pain and that too in detail.
I told him my story of
my suffering trapped in "the mother's day."

He told me my place was created
and I had to only step up and be in it.
I slept in tears and expired words
and woke up to send him a gift.

In turn he asked me to look
and hear a bell outside my window.
I waited and finally heard it.
It was an out-of-body experience.

Something happened, and my heart
instantaneously started beating differently,
for I had finally received the gift
from my God and my Superman.

I tried to shout out,
but to most I sounded a little off.
So I thought I will keep the secret
just to myself for me to remind me of him.

What a blessed day it has been,
for I have finally got to hear from him.
I really feel I need to dream
and in my dream to meet him once again.

Into Silence Again

76

I thought, *I am in a new world.*
But it's more of the same.
The real world bullies
creep into my private space.

So I go into silence forever
and decide that I will never open again ever.
Maybe this is my destiny
and I will close again infinitely.

Thank you world and my God,
for you have decided to turn a blind eye.
Never mind that I have nothing to lose.
You just took away what I had to reduce.

Forever I go in silence
and don't wait for your appearance.
That is why I am in isolation,
as this is the way I deal with it.

Me and My Hot Ginger Tea

It's 5:04 p.m., and I am sitting at my dining table
sipping a cup of my favorite hot ginger tea.
When I think of you,
you remind me of certainty.

For everything may fall apart,
but you will be always handy.
Your recipe is just so simple:
One thumb ginger into one cup water.

Add to it one and a half teaspoons black tea.
Well I use Splenda to be sugar free.
Bring it all to a boil.
And it's really not a toil.

When the water is bubbling with joy,
pour some milk in it and enjoy.
I never run out of ginger or black tea.
It's because I love you so much and you agree.

With the ups and downs in my life,
you are the one standing by my side.
When I think of you, my hot ginger tea,
you remind me of certainty.

Potty Training My Kid

Potty training is all about commitment.
We almost thought that my kid was ready.
But one small mistake threw it all apart.
One day I saw him go on the carpet upstairs and I was mad.
But it's gonna be all right.
We are gonna get there.

It's like I committed the biggest mistake.
After that, we both are in the square one.
I reintroduced diapers to spend some time on the Internet.
That was the second gravest mistake.
It's like I am in a chain reaction of mistakes.
But it's gonna be all right.
We are gonna get there.

So I am retraining myself from square one.
Looking up some more videos to keep up
and have hidden his diapers and brought out his pants.
Hopefully, this exercise should bring us back on track.
But it's gonna be all right.
We are gonna get there.

It's like I am juggling so many things at once,
keeping hope that nothing will fall apart.
So I need to be well balanced
and to just keep moving with tiny steps.
But it's gonna be all right.
We are gonna get there.

So I say to myself,

The Battle is not lost; there is still some time.

The emphasis is on staying committed and staying positive.

That's two things I need to keep focus on.

But it's gonna be all right.

We are gonna get there.

My Wish

79

It's 7:32 p.m., and I am sending out this prayer to you.
Dear God, this is my wish:

Please help me understand
the difference between my friend and foe.
Please send me the right opportunity
where I can bloom and not be in doom.

Please give me what I deserve
and what you think I have earned.
I need nothing more nor less.
Send me exactly what I have lived.

For only you know who I have been,
the righteous person as much as I could have seen.
Grant me a job where I can
show myself and be kind.

Where my boss is just an extension
of the God within me and doesn't create any confusion.
Help me get out of this rut.
And help me show my gut.

I just need to go outside
and be among people to show my real side.
Please bring upon your justice,
for you know that has always been my practice.

Help me secure an opportunity
where I am guarded by your angels,
Where I know you can keep an eye on me
just till the time I can stand on my feet.

Help me stand again,
and your pursuit will not be in vain.
I hope and pray once again
that you will help me see my way.

I want to be busy and not bored,
and I want to be happy and not sad.
Here is my prayer to you this evening:
grant me my wish and help me see it.

I Found My Way

It's 11:50 a.m., and I have to write this,
as I found my way.
There is nothing stopping me,
as I now know it's only me.

How much action I take
will determine where I go or stay.
So I unlock myself from this cage
and set myself free without any rage.

Thanks to this blogging
I stepped out of fogging.
I wrote my worries and cried my tears,
and I now have no fears.

All in all a great exercise,
and I am now more precise.
I now have a radical self-manifesto,
which is action, action, and more action.

I am neither sad nor low.
I am just bored.
As I take my actions again,
I hope to break free of this cage.
and never enter it,
as I found my way.

I Spoke with the Divine

81

It's 6.30 p.m. Sunday, and I need to write this.
I am very excited,
as I spoke with the divine.

Woke this morning to a glorious day,
stepped out, sat on the staircase
in the purple shade of the plum tree.

Did the usual chores,
finished lunch, and went upstairs
into my space to explore.

Don't know what happened,
but suddenly I closed my eye
and went into deep slumber high.

In my dream, I went on an excursion
with two elderly women,
and how amazing the whole thing was, intense.

It was a couple of minutes back, when I think
that I saw him speak to me,
and I knew it was the divine.

He said to me, "Let go of them,"
and he continued, "Let them be."
as soon as he said that, the women disappeared.

And there came a light again.
I saw it bright again.
And as I lay in my sleep, I understood what he said.

So I say to my bullies,
"I love you and I forgive you,
for I know you are guilty.

Don't have this fear, and don't be so insecure
For there is nothing I want from you.
I am just letting you go.

You rejected the God in me,
but I cherish the God in you
and hope he takes good care of you.

I cannot further hold on to this thread.
I release it
so that I can spread.

Here I go again, one more victory
and two more friends.
That's how my life has been.

Every time you put me through an event,
I will just take your lessons
and then add to my extension."

There is nothing holding me back,
I say to myself
as I see the divine light again.

On Earth Day today, you met me,
and you gave me a present.
How wonderful, and I think my life well spent.

I called for you, and you really came.
I think my connection with you
has been long due.

As I woke up to the sound of crushing ice,
I hear my hubby fiddling in the kitchen
and making a smoothie.

So I quickly run down to help,
and he says he sees a halo on my head
and a glow on my face.

There I go again; one fine
conversation with the divine
and I am back to light again.

It's 6.55 p.m., and so I end here with the note.
I serve the God in you,
and you serve the God in me.
Together we will make good company.

No More Excuses

82

It's 11:58 p.m., and I am not in a great mood.
But I have to get this out of my system.
No more excuses.

I will find my way.
I am not lost.
No more excuses.

I see God in people
and see people helping me.
No more excuses.

When I thought about him,
he sent me an e-mail.
So no more excuses.

My life is my own.
I am the doer and the beneficiary.
So no more excuses.

I am not lost, confused, or stuck.
I am here alive and striving.
So no more excuses.

I will make it happen
and bring a smile that I want.
So no more excuses.

I will take every chance,
pick every phone call, answer every e-mail.
So no more excuses.

I stop myself from dwelling on the bad memories
and giving myself food for thought.
So no more excuses.

I will only look for light,
and I will stick to it when I find it.
So no more excuses.

Everything will be all right,
I say to myself,
for when I called he answered.

It's 12:04 a.m., and I am going to sleep,
wishing someone a happy journey
and myself a great sleep.

God, Please Help Me Transcend My Dreams

It's 9:48 p.m. Friday night while I ponder my dreams.
God, please lift me off these petty issues
of day-to-day life.
Please help me transcend.

God, please help me cross off my worry list
and clinging life.
Please help me transcend.

I do not belong to this world
where everyone is so self-centered.
Please help me transcend.

God, you gave me Mother Teresa's heart.
Now give me the vision of Dr.Abdul Kalam.
Please help me transcend.

I don't belong among these minor fires.
Put me in the forefront of a world
where I can drive real change.

God, give me the strength to stick to my dreams
and build a fire in them
till they come true.

I roar into the open sky now
with hope in my eyes.
Please help me transcend.

God, please come and stand behind me,
for I am so alone in my situation.
I need your backing.

I am suffering with greatness,
and I have already started to morph into
someone I don't know.

Show me the way, God.
I am waiting for your hand
to hold me and help me find my way.

God, please bless me
and help me show my back to all my bullies,
and let there be no fear.

God, you are here,
I know. I hear you in people and see you in my child.
Please help me transcend.

I have suffered enough.
Lift me off this regular life.
Put me in a spot where I can see my way.

God, please bless me.
Show me the way.
I cannot stop my greatness.

God, please bless me.

Show me your face.

My Confidence

It's 12:24 a.m., and I am still not sleepy,
so I am going to crack down
on how to get back my confidence.

As my mental chatter continues,
I think about where my confidence went.
Did I lose it?

I think, *No.*
I just need to bring it out back.
Maybe I lose a little weight for that.

Or maybe I buy couple of new dresses
that fit better, or maybe
I buy a couple of new shades of lipsticks.

But I know confidence has
little to do with the exterior,
for I am missing something inside me.

Maybe I kept quiet
and didn't share my story.
That's what ate my confidence.

Or maybe someone intentionally
broke it by picking on points that hurt me.
I think that's more relevant.

But does that take away my confidence?
I bet no. Then why am I cribbing about it and
sobbing about me?

Damn, I just realized that
I didn't lose my confidence.
I am just unwilling to show it.

I feel sad and feel betrayed.
But does that shake my confidence?
I don't think so.

I don't want anyone to validate
my story or my part.
I don't care for validation.

I don't want anyone to sympathize
with me and my role.
I don't care about sympathy.

So what do I really care about
that I am missing?
Maybe I am missing the chance to show my passion.

That's what is killing me.
Maybe I expected so much from this place
and my dreams stopped flowing.

The flow discontinued
when I experienced some bad energies,
so I made a decision and quit.

And I did great.
I did myself a favor, as the energy was not good for me,
and I am now so much better.

So I own my decision.
I own all my decisions in my life,
and I own the consequences too.

I have nothing to hide,
nor nothing to complain.
So what if I have a couple pounds to lose.

Look at Oprah.
Did it stop her? No, damn no.
So why I am I cribbing about it?

I found the answer.
My confidence is right here
inside me, and much better than before.

For better things are happening.
I met God, and I met my mentor.
It's like the whole universe is conspiring.

Ask and you shall receive.
Give and you shall get.
That has always been my philosophy since I was little.

So did I give confidence to someone?
Yes, I did.
Maybe I need to give more.

God, please give me the confidence
of the mighty sun
to rise every morning and set when the time comes.

For I will give equal and more confidence
to someone who might ask if of me;
for I will always give more than receive.

Got it. I just remembered my own philosophy:
ask and you shall receive,
and give and you shall get.

No wonder, God, you put me through all this.
For I forgot my own principles.
Now I get it; it all falls into place.

It's 12:55 a.m. with that decision,
I decide that I am confident,
and I decide to give more.

I Won't Fall Apart

It's 7:33 p.m., and a day has gone by doing usual chores,
steam cleaned the floor, washed the dishes, folded laundry,
and I won't fall apart.

My eyes are still swollen,
and my head is foggy from yesterday's sadness.
But I won't fall apart.

Hubby reminded me that neither
Superman nor Romeo is gonna save me,
and I won't fall apart.

As I pull myself from my grave,
one more time I say to myself,
And I won't fall apart.

Even if I am a tiny fish in this town,
I am not a coward,
and I won't fall apart.

I pull my millions of pieces
together again and restart,
and I won't fall apart.

I don't have to sell myself
to misery and sympathy,
and I won't fall apart.

They think they crushed me,
but I am still alive,
and I won't fall apart.

They think they shut me down,
but here is my voice,
and I won't fall apart.

I will rise again and grow
to an influence and show,
and I won't fall apart.

I will cut scandals with niceness,
sabotage with goodness,
and I won't fall apart.

I will show what a tiny goodness
can do, and you'll remember,
and I won't fall apart.

For it takes much more to be right
than wrong, and that's what makes me strong,
and I won't fall apart.

For you may have influence
and power to kill my voice,
but I won't fall apart.

Right will always be right.
Truth will always remain,
and I won't fall apart.

I won't kill myself
and waste time sympathizing over something
that's not in my hand.

Drop by drop I will fuel myself
and shine right in front of you,
and you will remember.

My head, my heart, and my soul
are always in the right place.
I will get my confidence too.

You cannot crush me, you shark.
Remember those times
when you were a tiny fish too.

I will find my way
in this crowd, and I will survive,
and I won't fall apart.

You cut my wings
and put me in a cage and thought I died,
and I won't fall apart.

What you didn't see
is that you touched the angel,
and now the gods are really mad.

I forgive you before they come
and crack your guts,
and I won't fall apart.

Bit by bit I will grow,
and drop by drop I will fill
my life with power and strength.

One more time I pick myself from my grave,
and here I am full again,
and I won't fall apart.

I will wait for the perfect job and
not jump into something just for the heck,
and I won't fall apart.

God, give me the strength
and fuel to keep running in the right direction,
and I won't fall apart.

My story is of strength and survival.
I will burn the tears in my eyes,
but I won't fall apart.

I make a promise to myself today:
no more tears, no more fears,
and I won't fall apart.

If you pull my finger, I will grab your hand.
If you push me, I will pull the ground underneath you,
but I won't fall apart.

No more of your stalking.
You fool, spend your time wisely,
and I won't fall apart.

Take your chance while I forgive you
before I open my third eye,
and I won't fall apart.

It's 9:00 p.m., but I don't feel like going to the gym.
I will sit back and relax,
maybe eat a full dinner.

Change Please Come

It's 11:26 p.m. as I ponder it.
I met with my friend today.
She seemed far too distressed, and
within minutes I came home
with the same bug.

I quickly wrote a page
about my sorrows and pain,
and I closed myself again.

Then I got a magic call from
someone who asked me to
open my heart again.

Now I understand.
It takes a minute to fall,
but it takes a while for someone to pick you up.

I have covered far too many miles
to fall into darkness again,
so I reject to catch the misery bug.

There I go again,
singing my love song
and dancing myself to the gym again.

Here I am doing my regular thing,
writing my love story
with my dancing fingers.

I shift deleted the page with my pains
and felt so light
that I saw the grace again.

Here I am reliving my fairy tale
and waiting for change
to unfreeze me from my palace.

I have covered far too much ground
to look back or stop,
and all I can do is wait.

Change please come,
for I am waiting to see you.
Please unlock me of my inhibitions.

I am a river running toward the ocean.
All I want is speed
and the drift toward the right direction.

Change please come
like Romeo and lift me off my feet
and help me break my silence.

Everything Is History from Today

A new day begins; a new me begins.
I create a new future for me today.
Here is my dream that I will never let
anyone take away from me.

I start with one day at a time,
one baby step at a time.
Nobody knows what I am going through now.
I want to break away from my skin
like the caterpillar frees itself
from the cocoon and flies away.

As a beautiful butterfly,
fly away in the beautiful garden,
where I see colorful flowers,
red, yellow, pink, and purple,
and sing with the wind.

I wanna dance with love again.
I decide to cast off my cocoon.
No more am I going to eat away
my life inside my cocoon.
Here I break free and join the world
again.

One baby step at a time.
I might slip; I might fall.
But I will never stop
spreading my wings again.
World here I come, with my wide
and beautiful wings.

Jumping from flower to flower
in the sun and in the midst
of the beauty of nature,
I want to learn from the birds,
the bees, the trees, and the grass.

Meet with other colorful butterflies
and sing along a new song,
which will never be forgotten,
and I will never be a nobody anymore.

Today I free myself of my cocoon
and spread my wings
and decide that I am never ever
gonna go back into it.
Everything is history from today.

Where Are You, Superman?

There are times when I think of you,
times when I am so in need
to see one glimpse of you.

I have heard great stories of you
and hear that you help those in need.
Can I see you too?

I always longed for an elder brother
and thought that he would have
been just like you.

I sometimes wonder if I could fly
with you and save the world
just like you do.

Sometimes fly with you
and just see the world
from a bird's-eye view.

Sometimes I think you could
make me invisible and
I could play hide and seek with you.

Mostly I wonder if at the times
when I am fearful and worried
you could come and protect me.

I think you can teach me
some of your magic tricks,
which I can learn and use to make kids chuckle.

I could save lives too, you know,
and you smile and say to me,
"Look at what you did to yourself trying to."

These days I think of you often.
Life would have been much easier
if you could keep an eye on me.

Your little angel has been in trouble.
You would smile and say, "Not again.
I am busy saving the world."

I am sure there are too many miseries
that have taken your time.
But I just need to see your sign.

Show me a sign that I will be fine
and that your little angel
will dance again with joy and shine.

I see myself flying like a butterfly.
but I fear the bullies
who want to trap me again.

My troubles are not too big,
but I want to feel safe and secure.
Please break the teeth of bad intentions and cure.

Let's fly one day and sit
upon the tallest mountain and chat
and see the world through magic glasses.

These days I think of you often
Where are you, Superman?
Show me a sign that I will be fine.

Just Breathe

As I open my palms
and look at them
and put them on my face,
I say to myself,
Just breathe.

As I close my eyes
and look into the sky
of my mind
and touch that star,
I say to myself,
Just breathe.

As I curve my lips
and smile at the light
across the room
and gaze around,
I say to myself,
Just breathe.

As I see myself
in my mind's eye.
I see a beautiful butterfly
and stop and smile,
and I say to myself,
Just breathe.

As I think of God
I see hope and dreams
and thank all of them,
and I say to myself,
Just breathe.

Everything will be all right
once again.
Just be patient,
and I say to myself,
Just breathe.

The Spring Sun

What a lovely spring day it was
as I wake from my sleep.
I went out my front door
and sat myself on the staircase
where the sun was shining
and beaming its joy
onto my cheeks.

I sat in the shade of the plum tree
whose leaves were shiny purple,
and gazed around at the beautiful weather.
Oh God, thank you
for the spring sun.

Spring reminds me of beautiful
flowers, trees, rivers, and bees.
Spring reminds me of joy.
The spring sun reminds
me of the hope that
God is here to share his glory
with the insignificant me.

I was kissed by the spring sun,
and I couldn't stop blushing.
Thank you nature
for pouring your warmth
in my heart and enlightening me.

Little Girl Sitting on the Mango Tree

When I was a little girl,
I remember myself sitting perched
on a the branch of my favorite mango tree.

How beautiful was that moment
in the middle of nature,
all quiet, and the only sounds that mattered
were the ones coming from the sweet birds.

I sat there on Saturdays and Sundays,
usually in the afternoons
when all the other kids
were napping in their beds.

All summer I spent climbing
to spots showing me a new perspective
of what was under the tree
and in the garden.
I sat there sometimes chewing on peanuts,
sometimes on sugarcane,
or sometimes just eating the juicy mangoes
that the tree gave itself.
How eternal were those times
of peace and quiet and solitude.

Butterflies and birds talked to me.
I loved the sunlight creeping through,
the leafy branches and
enlightening my moments of total bliss.

I love those days,
when I was a little girl sitting
on a the branch of my favorite mango tree.

No More Excuses

It's 11:58 p.m., and I am not in a great mood.
But I have to get this out of my system.
No more excuses.

I will find my way.
I am not lost.
No more excuses.

I see God in people
and see people helping me.
No more excuses.

When I thought about him,
he sent me an e-mail.
So no more excuses.

My life is my own.
I am the doer and the beneficiary.
So no more excuses.

I am not lost, confused, or stuck.
I am here alive and striving.
So no more excuses.

I will make it happen
and bring a smile that I want.
So no more excuses.

I will take every chance,
pick every phone call, answer every e-mail.
So no more excuses.

I stop myself from dwelling on the bad memories
and giving myself food for thought.
So no more excuses.

I will only look for light
and I will stick to it when I find it.
So no more excuses.

Everything will be all right,
I say to myself,
for when I called he answered.

It's 12:04 a.m., and I am going to sleep,
wishing someone a happy journey
and myself a great sleep.

Bully Strikes Again

93

4:24 p.m. I just woke up from my little nap
and saw a couple of messages,
and I see the bully at work again.

So here's to you, my bully.
You enjoy your stay here,
for I will close myself forever again.

I know you are much smarter than me,
for I don't have a brain that works like yours,
and you brought tears in my eyes again.

Three cheers to you, my bully,
as you win again.
This is the exact reason that makes you a devil.

No more of this bullying.
I forgive you, again, you fool.
Just remember you can never bring me down.

Romeo Please Save Me; I Feel So Alone

94

I tried my best,
but I still feel so alone.
I feel like I don't fit in,
for I cannot be happy here.

I am lost in the middle of nowhere.
Neither tea nor this writing brings me calm.
I think I am slipping into darkness again
when I remember those things.

Please fade away those memories
and wipe out the blues,
for I spent the whole day in tears
When I thought about my fears.

I cannot do this anymore,
for I have to stop it somewhere.
I need to be out of this place
to feel alive again.

I cannot live in this cycle
waiting for something to happen,
Maybe I just need to sleep
and hope my sadness goes away in a beep.

Come take me away
far to some wonderland
where there is no wait,
no watch, and no chase.

I just want to smile
and hope to feel alive again.

The Story of the Goldfish and the Sharks

95

Once upon a time not too long ago
there came a tiny goldfish from far away
who was very joyful, excited, and fun loving.

The goldfish started working at a new tank.
Didn't understand so asked a big brown shark.
He looked calm and quiet.

A big cruel white shark thought that the goldfish complained
and started chasing the little one
till it was out of breath.

Then came a jealous brown shark wearing a goldfish mask.
The goldfish emptied her heart
and told her what she felt.

This deceiving brown shark went and changed the story
and told the big brown shark,
and life for the goldfish became even dark.

Now the tiny goldfish didn't understand
whom to trust and whom to not,
as everyone was wearing a big fat mask.

So the tiny goldfish kept coming in every day
and doing her work and secretly shedding tears
but found it extremely hard.

What the goldfish didn't tell anyone
was that she was getting harassing calls
on her landline.

One day the goldfish was gifted a box
with the identification of her family's whereabouts,
And the tiny fish got scared.

The goldfish changed her phone number
but got a call on the new phone too.
Then she was lost.

She and her family went on vacation
thinking things will get better,
but the same thing continued thereafter.

A big black shark said he would kill,
and the big cruel white shark asked for the goldfish's baby.
The goldfish couldn't breathe anymore.

All was the play of a big fat white ugly shark,
who was sitting at the top
but was wearing a mask.

The tiny goldfish got anxious and was scared.
But they wouldn't care,
as the work was produced with flying colors.

The tiny goldfish didn't know whom to trust,
the brown sharks or the white sharks,
as both were attacking.

So one day the tiny goldfish just
broke free from the tank
and ran to her safe haven.

As a consequence, the tiny fish doesn't trust anyone,
because she thinks everyone is a shark
wearing a mask.

But the tiny goldfish is not so stupid.
She can see through these lessons
and wait and watch for good times.

My Magic Mentor

It is 11:45 a.m., and I am finally free to write.
I met with him finally,
and it was a cake walk.

I was so nervous until yesterday.
But I woke up at 6:00 a.m. with so much joy
that I knew I was okay.

We met over breakfast,
and I was so happy at last.
I think I will be okay.

I wanted to be so open with him
that I spilled my beans
with no restrictions.

The first thing I told him
was the one thing I was most afraid of,
and I killed it. It feels so light.

Looks like it was a plot played
by the universe
to set the right order with what I got.

I hope he sees the spark in me
and likes me for what I am
and what I am able to become.

I know nothing comes easy
This was one of those things,
but my wait was not in vain.

I felt he looked right through me
as if he knew all about me,
and that's just the thing I like.

I like everyone who can see
through the barriers of my exterior
into the tiny flame inside my interior.

I am very happy that this day has finally come
and I am all done.
Yes, I know all will be all right.

I was so tempted to tell him
my story of the tiny goldfish
and the sharks, but I said it was just "company culture."

I was so tempted to tell him
how bullied I was at my last thing,
but I just referred to it as my needing more exposure.

I think he understood it
without me speaking much about it.
I hope he does.

How can I tell him
that I am the tiny goldfish hiding in the bushes,
for I am afraid of the sharks.

But as he said, I will learn my way.
And I believe it.
That's the only way one can survive the day.

He showed me some lovely photos.
I couldn't imagine how beautiful
the place must have been in itself.

I gave him a small gift,
a book called *What Matters Now,*
and hope it gives his busy day a lift.

All in all a lovely meeting,
as I long waited
to see my magic mentor.

It's 12:10 p.m., and I am back to my chores.
I think I am going for two loads of laundry and one of dishes
and writing a card for my friend who just had a baby.

What Are My Talents?

97

It's 2:20 p.m., and my baby is still up
and my home is in a mess,
but I have to think this out loud.

What are my talents?

I am good at reading a book
and summarizing into a single sentence.

I am great at writing and can finish
a book overnight.

I love to talk to people
and within seconds know their authentic side.

I love to travel and see
the beauty of nature and the world.

I like to see technology
and how it changes the man to be more human.

I like to cheer people up.
For I know that everyone has a real story of struggle.

Mostly I feel like I am good
at everything the world wants, but do I want that?

I love to learn how people lead
and what make them great lions in a herd.

I love to learn what ignites their sparks
and what fuels their engines.

What I am really good at
is that I understand people at a level that they don't catch.

I can basically learn a new language
within days and speak the same.

I can learn a new concept and apply it
in its very unique fashion.

I can take the drama out of articles
and just give it to you in a gist.

I can listen to and hear different things,
but I can understand only what is correct.

I see imaginary patterns and see the flow
and catch the outliers in bright daylight or in a dim glow.

My life has always been all about my love to learn
and to be a student for life.

Mostly I am in search of someone
who can guide me to the right direction.

The Scale Has Finally Tipped

98

It's 10:40 p.m. back from the gym, and I am bubbling with joy
as the scale has finally tipped
and there goes another four pounds on the fly.

Wow, I already feel so light
and also feel a spring in my walk.
I am so glad to talk.

Let's talk about something fun
of going to the gym and run,
for good days have finally come.

The next thing for me is
I want to copy my hubby and run
a big marathon.

Just saw an ad for a Susan G. Kommen walk.
Maybe that's the one
I need to put down with a chalk.

I cannot wait to wear the pink T-shirt
and flaunt my new better self,
but I do need more help.

I had signed up for a personal trainer
when I enrolled
but didn't use it, as I knew I cannot afford.

But I now plan to start training
for a big marathon,
and everything will fall in place and catch on.

This is just a drop in the sea.
I have so much more to lose,
for it has taken me three years to get here and choose.

But I am now on track
and it's just a matter of time.
I feel like I am getting back.

Three cheers to me in my name
for sticking to the routine
and killing it in the gym again.

My Dear Bully

It's 1:45 p.m. as I rush out of my bath.
Didn't dress, since I would lose my words.
and I have to write this for you.

I was supposed to shop for a new dress,
and here I am shedding tears,
and I have to write this for you.

You remind me of the pain and open my scars.
But I am here to punch you in your face,
and I have to write this for you.

What do you know about my character,
for I have taken several births
before I became so pure.

Ask the white rose, ask the sweet bird,
and ask them to go around
and show me one soul so true and pure.

You could only scare me to kill myself.
But here I am alive not once but twice,
and I have to write this for you.

If I wanted I could crush you
and put you between heaven and hell,
and you would pray for hell.

But I can only create.
I can never harm even if you are the devil,
for my powers are only for the good.

As I open myself, I dare you
to scare me again, and I will punch you in the face,
for you don't know my greatness

I am here to fix the world,
so you dare to stop me
and belittle me. You insignificant soul.

I hug to steal someone's pain,
and I kiss the snake to take away his venom.
What do you know about me?

When I am feeling wanting to die
I motivate someone to live a life.
What do you know about me?

I secretly worry about the world,
for there are so few heroes.
What do you know about me?

I realized my greatness when I was three
and I tried to fix the broken with my little fingers.
What do you know about me?

I dream of love and hope and care
about the change in the world
to get it in the right flow.

Don't do you dare try to stop me again,
for there are three souls keeping an eye on you:
my lost son, my secret lover, and my Superman.

If I wanted I could ask the gods
to crush you with their toes.
But instead I asked mercy for you.

What you don't know is that
I have forgiven you long back.
I don't even think of you anymore.

I cannot hate you, for you taught me so much.
Every time you cut me, I grew.
I am so strong cuz of you.

You know very little about me,
you insignificant soul.
For it has taken me many births to be so perfect.

I can only give and heal, so here's another chance.
Take it and clean your mess.
That's the only way to your solace.

Watch everything you think
and say about me, for I now have all the gods
on my side; you understand that.

Here is my forgiveness.
Take it and run, for it's the last time
I am in the mood to give it.

It's 2:37 p.m. on Saturday, and I have to run,
for I need to buy my beautiful dress
to meet the new me.

Topics to Discuss

It's 5:06 p.m. on Monday, and I have only a day
before I meet him.
So what do I want to discuss with him?

Maybe ask him how he became so successful?
And then ask him
how can I be too.

What does he look for in people
that he likes,
and maybe I can showcase that too.

Ask him what motivates him
and gives him his drive,
and maybe I can learn too.

Ask him how it feels to be in the spotlight
and shine in the frontline,
and maybe I can dream that too.

Ask him if he ever felt confused or stuck
and who guided him,
and maybe I can get that direction too.

Ask him what qualities he cherishes
in himself that his team appreciates,
and maybe I can practice those too.

Ask him about his interests.
I know he likes photography,
and maybe I can show some of my pics too.

Maybe discuss places I have been in Germany
and cities I loved
and hope to reconnect with those moments.

On that topic, let me look at my photos
and remind myself of the spots
I traveled to ages ago.

If he likes photography, then he likes nature,
and what a perfect thing.
It makes me smile.

What I really want to ask him
Is whether he likes anything about me.
But I know I won't ask this ever.

Mostly I want to discuss topics he likes,
because I want him to be in his element
and show me his magic smile.

It's 5:26 p.m., and let me continue this again
for now I am off into the kitchen
to make some hot ginger tea.

Don't Know What to Write Today

It's 11:30 p.m., and I am still logged on.
It's raining outside today;
weather is a little cold.
But I don't know what to write today.

Feels like I fell in love again
or caught the happiness bug.
Something happened,
and I want to smile again.

Funny what is happening to me.
But it feels like time is passing by
and I am unable to keep up, but still
I am singing songs again.

I was supposed to be spending
all my time looking for jobs.
But I spent the whole day
looking at my fave romantic songs.

Did God put me back in time
to rewrite my story?
Did he give me another chance
to create a new fairy tale?

In this fairy tale, I don't want to be
the princess or the prince.
I want to be the fairy with the magic wand
and sprinkle some magic fairy dust.

I want to be the secret angel
who always brings people together,
brings on smiles,
and brightens people's lives.

I want to wipe out cries
and spread happiness,
spread magic without anybody
knowing who did it.

I want to reach every lonely heart
and tell them that they are not alone
and that they are taken care of
by someone who they don't know.

God, make me the secret angel
so I can fix the world
and leave it a better place
for all the babies to come.

Please give me the beauty of the angel,
the heart of the mother,
the strength of a brother,
and the joy of a baby.

It's 11:43 p.m., and I am feeling sleepy.
I need to dream
and spread joy in my world.
So good night world; see you tomorrow.
Don't know what to write today.

God Grant Me the Serenity

With this message I touch your feet
to seek your blessings today.
I have put my heart into these words
as I set my heart again on something.
Will it break again?

God, please prepare me
to accept the life as it comes
and to control the things I can,
for I have and I am trying to do my part.
The rest is in your hands.

I don't know what is good for me.
That is why I fear to ask.
Send me your blessings
and keep me in line with your task.

I have gone through the whole circle
and seen both the sides of the coin.
What else is there for me to learn,
as I have lived your lessons for so long?

Show me the light one more time,
and I will take it from there.
Help me lead all those
who have lived and learned their way.

Show me how to differentiate
between the good and the bad,
for I have too little trust,
as I have burned my hands with both.

I need your special blessings today
sending you my prayers again.
Please don't think this a bribe,
for only you know I have paid for everything.

Please send me a special call
and let me hear your voice through them.
Leave me a message,
and I will think it's Superman.

Stupid Fat

It's 11:12 p.m., and I just got free to write.
I went to the gym to just find out
that I had gained two out of the four lost.

So I decided to shoot my stupid fat.

You always come uninvited
and stay beyond your welcome.
You are my stupid fat.

I find it difficult why you
think I don't know the ground rules.
You are my stupid fat.

You hide in places that are obvious
and stick there for a while.
You are my stupid fat.

Why can't you relocate
and show yourself a new fate.
You are my stupid fat.

You always show up in the wrong places
with untimely and unintentional faces.
You are my stupid fat.

I already won one battle with you
when I saw you run for help.
You are my stupid fat.

So I take that knowledge from my last conquest
and hit you with a bat at best.
You are my stupid fat.

I am going to melt you on the elliptical,
burn you on the bicycle.
You are my stupid fat.

If you are still stubborn,
I will scorch you in the sun during my run.
You are my stupid fat.

I plan to run a marathon,
so you'd better get ready, you python.
You are my stupid fat.

For I am going to have to part with you
and wish you farewell.
You are my stupid fat.

If you be nice to me.
I will let you hide in the right places.
You are my stupid fat.

I have a new strategy
to burn you with my newfound energy.
You are my stupid fat.

You are not welcome anymore,
for I let you stay too long.
It's now time to say good-bye.

You are my stupid fat.

It's 11:25 p.m., and that's it. I am just a little
bit frustrated over gaining some weight back.
But I can understand; I have to work even
harder and control my diet

Recovery Plan

As I come out of depression,
I use my recovery plan
and will identify negative thoughts
that contribute to my illness.

As I come out of depression,
I will use thought stopping
to block the negative thoughts
and join a support group.

As I come out of depression,
I will use "I-statements"
to be more precise about my needs
and communicate with people better.

As I come out of depression,
I will concentrate and focus better
by learning and practicing meditation
and deep breathing for relaxtion.

As I come out of depression,
I will set healthy boundaries
and know whom to approach for what
and be compassionate about myself.

As I come out of depression,
I decide to take a break
and go to my favorite holiday destination,
enjoying the beach and the sun.

A Beautiful Hummingbird

A beautiful hummingbird
once came to me
and said that I am so kind.
So I try to be more kind.

A beautiful hummingbird
once came to be
and said that I am so happy.
So I try to be more happy.

A beautiful hummingbird
once came to me
and said that I was so lovely.
So I try to be more lovely.

A beautiful hummingbird
once came to me
and said I am beautiful.
So I try to be more beautiful.

No Shame

There is no shame in
being depressed
and finding oneself and
fighting mental illness.

Like all diseases,
mental illness also is a disease
that needs treatment
with pills and skills.

Free yourself of the burden
of hiding from everyone;
go ahead and share
that you are in battle.

Get as much as helps
from family and friends
and loved ones
to battle with darkness.

Medicine

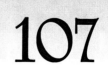

At first I rejected it.
But now I have accepted it
to help fix my depression.
Medication is my friend.

Had some side effects,
sleepiness and heaviness,
but now it feels better.
Medication is my friend.

It takes several trials
before a perfect dose is effective
without any major side effects.
Medication is my friend.

Now I can catch up with life
powered by my medication
and skills to learn
and enjoy life.

I Don't Want

I don't want to be
the last one to forgive.

I don't want to be
the last one to hold on to grudge.

I don't want to be
the last one the give up their story.

I don't want to be
the last one to accept the reality.

I don't want to be
the last one to give up isolation.

I don't want to be
the last one to be honest with myself.

I don't want to be
the last one to be forgiven.

CPSIA information can be obtained at www.ICGtesting.com
Printed in the USA
BVOW05s2025131114

375036BV00001B/4/P